Thursdays at 2

Poems to Gladden
the Heart

by the West Bay Poets

edited by Tracy Lee Karner

Cover Art: Sunflower, by Cathy Keithan

Library of Congress cataloging-in-publication data:

Karner, Tracy Lee and West Bay Residential Services
Thursdays at 2: Poems to Gladden the Heart / Tracy Lee Karner
and West Bay Residential Services, Inc.
cm
ISBN 153350170x

1. Poetry 2. Expressive and Creative Arts--Poetry
3. Poetry Therapy

Published by Rose Hall Media Company, St. Cloud, Minnesota

rosehallmedia.com

Rose Hall
Media
Company

for Mark Brown

Use this book to write
collaborative poetry
with your group!

See page 74.
See page 74.

Contents

Biographies

Poets and Artists

LETTERS OF THE HEART
from US
to YOU

We are a circle of poets connected to West Bay Residential Services, a non-profit agency offering innovative living options, day and employment supports to individuals with intellectual and developmental disabilities.

There is no place a person with disabilities cannot go, when given the appropriate support. By using community resources--local poets, coffee shops, and libraries--we have learned to bring our unique, individual talents together in collaboration to make poems.

Poetry helps us appreciate the wonder, joy and love wrapped up in our daily experiences. It opens our eyes to the important, mysterious truth that although there may be superficial differences, in our essential humanity all of us are very much the same.

Poetry uses ordinary words, but strings them together in surprising ways, with images and metaphors. This opens up the inner world of the heart and helps us recognize ourselves in each other.

Poetry has enabled us to see and listen to one another more carefully, and this has built deeper, more respectful relationships among us. We are members of the richly diverse Rhode Island community of citizens. And our poetry has become our joyful song, which we want to share with you.

Thank you for taking the time to get to know us better.

Thursdays at 2
Poems

After hearing Christina Rosetti's poem "Clouds" (page 44), we set out to write a poem with the same title. We began with the question, "What do you see when you look at a cloud?" Someone said, "Old Man," and we started making up rhymes to the rhythm of Rosetti's poem. We thought it was funny when we ended up with a poem that is not about clouds at all. From this we learn that it's okay—and sometimes it's even better—when things don't turn out according to plan.

It's Not About Clouds

Old man, old man,
what color is your cane?
When it is gray,
it's going to rain.
When it is red,
it's time for bed.
Old man, old man,
what color is your cane?

One of the ways we make poems is to begin by collecting a list of rhyming words. Next, one of us picks a subject, and we try to use all the rhyming words in sentences about that subject. Each of us is thinking of his or her own experiences and memories. This makes the poem go along an unpredictable path.

Surprise is an important element of poetry. You might notice that Yosemite looks like it should fit into the rhyme scheme, (rhyming with kite) but its unexpected sound adds an eye-opening experience to this poem.

Red Kite

Light a kite, fly fire.
White moon, full of holes
we want you to shine.
Shine on our night
and let our hearts take flight.

Take us away on kite strings
to the amusement park,
the garden in Boston, or Yosemite.
The kite sails to enormous height
and we fly it.

Often we read aloud a published poem before we start creating. This serves as a springboard to poetic thinking. The following poem was inspired by Eliza Lee Follen's "The Good Mooly Cow" (page 45).

The Mee-owly Tiger Kitty

Here's a penny, you mee-owly Tiger Kitty.
Come, get a kite now
because it is summer and windy.
Be done with the yarn ball play
and the rat chasing the cake.
Fly away home, you
mee-owly Tiger Kitty.

We love snacks and trees
and flying red kites and green.
When you come again to see us
you mee-owly Tiger Kitty
bring your kite, leave the rat
and take a nap in the sun.

Repetition is an important tool of poetry. When four of us cele-brated birthdays on the same Thursday, we decided to write a poem repeating the happy word, "celebrate." So we gathered a list of images having to do with birthdays, and made this poem.

A Poem to Celebrate Birthdays

Let's celebrate balloons
the sound when they pop
when they fly up in the sky
when they're purple and red and blue
and yellow.

Celebrate M&M frosting.
Put it in the freezer
(they won't freeze as hard as you think—
your teeth won't break).

And celebrate milk
smooth like velvet
creamy like cake
soft as a kitty-cat.

Let's celebrate hugs, ooh, aah.
Hugs that taste like butterscotch and raindrops.
Hugs in the early morning
that smell like flowers
and look like clocks.

Let's celebrate birthdays
like we celebrate
Amen.

We enjoyed Dorothea Lasky's poem "Monsters." So we borrowed her line "There are monsters everywhere," and came up with our own poem, in which monsters are naughty, a little bit confrontational, delicious, and at the end of the day, reverent.

Monsters

There are monsters
everywhere. There are monsters...
Avon calling. There are monsters

in the cake, monsters on the phone.
There are monsters after the cat.
There are monsters in my sweater,

in my dreams, they stare at you,
at your friends. Cotton balls
can be made out of monsters.

They come out in the early mornings,
they feel like silk and frosted cake and fish fins.
They taste like sour patch kids.

They taste like coffee and cotton candy—
all at once in your mouth!
Monsters love the word Amen.

We are learning that to be poets, we must learn from Sherlock Holmes, who said, "Watson, you see but you do not observe." On a fine summer day, our visiting poet Helen D'Ordine (see page 60) asked us to observe strawberries, blueberries, cherries, watermelon and clementines. We examined, touched and tasted while our visiting poet wrote down our thoughts. And then she put our words all together like this:

SE-E-E-E-E, FE-E-E-E-EL, TA-A-A-A-ASTE

A strawberry with no straw,
red, heart-shaped
tiny yellow seeds, like commas.
Don't eat the grassy, green hat!!
Yummy, juicy! Stains my fingers.
Strawberry.

Can you find the
blueberry's secret star?
Purple and green inside.
Most are sweet, some sour.
Yummy good for you!
Blueberry.

Dark red and darker red,
the cherry is round.
Don't eat the stem!
Don't eat the pit!
Take a bite.
Stain your tongue.
Cherry.

Watery watermelon with
black seeds or white seeds.
Only eat the white ones!
Only eat the red fruit.
Stop at the white rind
and green skin!
Watermelon.

Clementine, cousin of the
orange and tangerine.
Peel the rough, wrinkly,
smooth or bumpy skin.
Eat the half moon, smiley pieces.
Chew it well. Don't choke!
Clementine.

Yummy, juicy, fruit!

None of us speaks German, except for one of our visiting poets, who read aloud to us the poem, "Du Bist Wie Eine Blume" (You are Like a Flower) by Heinrich Heine. After reading each line, Tracy asked us to tell her what we heard. The intention was not to translate, but to invent some kind of sense out of the strange sounds. In that exercise, we came up with this little fragment of a poem about the sadness of parting. Poetry has the power to make even melancholy things seem beautiful.

You are Like a Flower

It's time to go home.
You're all invited.
Your time is ended.

I hope it's beautiful.
Let me take a deep breath fast.
This means goodbye.

Here's what Billy Collins' poem "Litany" inspired during one winter session, when we were getting really tired of all the snow and ice. We focused on coming up with images: of winter and snow: of color (red); sound (people talking); and taste (yum! Chicken Parm!) And then we plugged all those images into a litany, which turned our frustration around. We became the snow and ice, and somehow that made us happier.

What We Are in Winter

We are the icicle and the slush.
We are the snow on the streets and on the palm trees.
We are the mother's rose, and the pillow drowsing on the bed.

However, we are not the music of people talking at Walmart,
or chicken parm, or the day room.
And there is no chance we could be the crayons.

But maybe we are the penguins hiding in arctic water,
or possibly the polar bear.
There is no way we will ever be the cars on the street at 2:00.

Our reflection in a frozen pond will show we are not the jacket
or the closet hibernating by the door.
Because this winter we prefer to be
the icicle, the slush, and the snow.

And another litany (a fancy word for "list"), this one inspired by Christopher Smart's poem from the 1700's which begins "For I will consider my cat, Jeoffry..."

Who We Are

We are brave
for we have fun in everything
for we laugh at everyone—we do!

We are friends;
we are family.
We do what we want to do.

We do what we are capable of doing
which is everything.
We love one another.

We are cats; we are lovebirds.
We are lions and tigers—we roar
for we eat too much.

We are cheerleaders;
we get in your face, for we like to
for we are brave.

We are not gullible, malleable
or contemptible, but we are sassy.
We shout in the streets.

We feel the beat, the boogie.
We build the drums.
We give you heartburn; so take a Tums.

We had fun talking about various statues in Rhode Island, and were delighted when our conversation ended on a pun (relief has two meanings: release from distress; and a technique used by sculptors). If you want to imagine how we made this poem, think of the blank spaces between lines as a cue that a new person is speaking. It sounds like a family of twelve telling a story, when everyone exuberantly adds to the conversation by interrupting the previous speaker.

Statues

There's a statue in Burnside Park—

Captain Burnside on his horse.

At Providence Place Mall there's a horse

in front of P.F. Chang.

There's a statue in Roger Williams Park

of the founder of Providence.

A statue on the State House

of the golden Independent Man.

They took him down to remake the dome

or to fix him up,

but Grandpa said he wasn't there because

he had to go to the bathroom.

Even statues need a little relief!

The poet laureate of New Hampshire, Alice B. Fogel, explains in her book Strange Terrain: A Poetry Handbook for the Reluctant Reader, *that some poems are about "the deep meaning of purely emotional sound." In other words, there may not be much going on in a poem other than the way it sounds.*

Using Fogel's poem "Sea Gull" as a model, we wanted to write a poem about a rhododendron that is mostly about the way the poem sounds. So first we talked about the word itself, with the beginning rhod-do rhyme, and the den - dron rhyme at its end. Then we examined clusters of Rhododendrons by sight, touch and smell. We pulled apart the blossoms, leaves and petals, talked about every plant part in detail, and wrote down our observations. Finally, our visiting poet assembled our word pictures into this poem.

Notice how many syllables nearly rhyme with dron; also a number of words have the "o" sound found in rhodo.

Rhododendron

It explodes open, fire like
    overnight   the bush in flames
its snowcone blooms
    are clusters of blossoms
fragile   like tissue paper.

They are like cups,   or little tulips.

Do the blossoms always grow in even numbers?
  ??

Each has 5 starlike petals, mostly purple
    with one group of yellow dots
  where the sun   and the rain
touched
    each flower in seeds
a thumbprint   of growth.

In the center are ten   magenta
    antenna   like fingers,
like bits of glowing sunset.

The leaves two-toned
    grass green on top
smooth waxy,
    the bottom a little
bit rough light green
    like spring.

Brown stems
    like pretzel sticks.
        Yum!
It's rhododendron time.

To find words for this poem, we examined treasures collected from the beach: jars filled with sand, ocean water and seaweed; shells; rocks; plants. We talked and wrote down our observation. Then we listened to the poem "Sunset" by Chinese Tung Dynasty poet Tu Fu (713-770), and worked to pattern our poem after his. We organized our observations into a series of images related to the title, then ended with a feeling of wonder, phrased as a question.

Beaches

Beaches award relaxation and peace.

Sea shells float in tides.

We ride the waves, search for sea glass.

Ocean whoosh-shush-shushes, rocks

us like a lullaby. Gold-gray

granite shimmers in the sunlight.

Seaweed billows like sheets on a clothesline.

Bathing suits and beach towels, purple sunset,

radios, sea grass, suntans--

a kaleidoscope of color.

Who knew a cool breeze could carry

all your worries away?

We return to one of poetry's oldest themes again and again, because the world can always use more love.

Dandelions and Roses

I love roses red.
I like Gerbera daisies.
Red roses, apples and hearts--
Love with your heart.

I love dandelions yellow,
Dandelion salad and dandelion wine.
When they get old and they turn white--
make a wish and blow.

Love with your heart.

Avid readers of American poetry might recognize that this next poem borrows the rhythm and cadence of the first, excessively long, sentence of Walt Whitman's well-known "Out of the Cradle, Endlessly Rocking."

The fact that we, like Whitman, end our poem with the word "sing" is entirely coincidental. Tracy Lee Karner (see page 63) didn't tell us that we were trying to sound like Walt Whitman, nor did she read his poem to us, until after we were all done writing our own poem. Most of us had never even heard of him.

She started with the question, "What do we do?" We answered, "Dance, smile, laugh and sing." Then we took a vote to see which of those words was our favorite to be the last word of our poem. Sing won—maybe because of its pretty sound.

This was one of those magical days when the poem seemed to come to us as something completely formed, when we all were "on the same page." Tracy asked questions, we answered, she wrote down everything we said, and when she stepped back to read our words, we were astonished.

Tracy did very little tweaking or rewriting with this poem. She merely broke the lines in a Whitmanesque fashion, and squeezed her words "imperfect" and "boistrous" into the last two lines.

Over the Blue Chair

Over the blue chair, powerfully wheeling,
Over the rabbit's hop, the soft thumping,
Over the pink mountain and down the ski slope,
   where the brothers and sisters, beyond the rainbow, circle
   and square dance together on stage,
   up from the red valley, smiling and laughing like friends,
Over the vines of purple grapes,
From the Greek and ancient Roman gods' voices,
From the memories of fathers and grandfathers,
From the great grandfathers and mothers,
From lands far away,
From millions and trillions of suns, shining on grassy knolls,
   warming the hearts of friends and family,
As cats meowing, purring, stretching,
A chorus, yet individual poets, smiling ourselves into the
   moment,
We, people enjoying each other, pleasers of the program,
Taking responsibility for our imperfect selves,
A boistrous blessing sing.

We love color! So when Ocean State Poet Carol Anderheggon (see page 51) spent time with us in October, 2015, we were delighted that she wanted us to use images of color to make haiku-like poems. Haiku is a Japanese form of three lines, traditionally broken into five, seven and five syllables. Strictness is something that doesn't always work for us, so we adapted the Japanese idea to make our own style of poems evoking images of color and nature. We chose our favorite colors, came up with images and ideas about them, and Carol then tweaked our words into these charming one-sentence poems.

Cycle of Life

Leaves, trees, grass and ivy
    consume soil, air, sunlight and rain
    to give us apples, grapes,
    lettuce, peppers and peas!

October

Waterfall shimmers and splashes,
    mirrors the yellow and red
    of the fall bushes and trees.

Red

We dress up in sexy red—
    lipstick, nail polish, blush and shoes,
    reminding us of tomatoes and strawberries.

The process and results of communal poetry writing have been so beneficial and satisfying, that we've taken our poetry-making sessions out into the community--to Senior Centers and coffee shops-- to share with Rhode Island. We hope to keep expanding our reach by inviting more people to join our public group sessions, and by teaching other groups and agencies how to use poetry-making as a community building exercise.

Here's a poem we made at one of our Coffee Shop Sessions. We began with the fantasy of what it would be like to own a coffee shop. Then we bought our coffee and tea, and while we enjoyed it, we talked about how our drinks looked, tasted, felt and smelled. Through this process we discovered that making poetry helps us be more attentive to, and appreciative of, the little blessings in our lives. Poetry encourages us to imagine a good future.

Coffee, Money and Poems

If we owned our own coffee shop
we'd sell coffee and get money.
We'd get paid. We'd buy jeans!
We could buy a radio, listen
to WHJY rock: Def
Leppard; Love Me Tender.
We'd drink coffee with our friends, eat
donuts, muffins, bacon-egg-and-cheese.

Coffee with milk is tan, feels smooth
to the throat going down, smells
like cinnamon and vanilla. Tea
is good, too, smells herby, steamy.
We'd rather have coffee but tea is cheaper.
So we want our own coffee shop—
to pay for our coffee; to own
a perfect place to make our poems.

And now a selection of poetry we've made on our own, without help of visiting poets. On this and the facing page are poems about nature (one of our favorite topics!) followed by two poems in rhyming couplets, a form we like a lot.

Birds

Birds flock in the summer
and gone by the winter
they come by the dozen.
They make babies to come in the summer.
We see many colors like rainbows.
They chirp in the morning,
like an alarm clock
still being dark.
They like to make messes,
sometimes on your head--
can mean good luck in the end!

Night Light

When the sun goes down
the sky turns black.
We look at the moon,
we pet our cats.
The world is sleeping
and all the stars come out.
The bats are dancing in the black night.
All the black sand is at night.
The sky is glowing.
The fireflies fly all night.

Autumn 2015

Kids go back to school and ride the bus.
It's work, work, work for the rest of us!

Children jump into leaves of yellow and gold
while adults rake and ache 'cause they're getting old.

Mom & Dad get to cut out the slime
while boys and girls eat yummy pumpkin seeds any time.

Trick or treaters get lots of Halloween treats--
Dads and Moms steal them when the kids are asleep.

Two adults being scared of the dark is a joke,
to a child it's trembling over witches and ghosts.

Parents won't let kids watch horror on TV
but if you ask Paul, he says "that's for me!"

A favorite treat for everyone is candy corn and kisses--
we'll eat those for dinner as one of our favorite dishes.

Kids play baseball and football with agility
while parents are couch potatoes--just watch it on TV.

No jackets for children--they'll play in the cold.
Adults bundle up more as they get old.

Heating bills make adults worry
while kids leave the lights on, always in a hurry.

We like cider and cocoa and pumpkin spice coffee
and gooey candy apples with sprinkles of toffee.

Having Ourselves a Merry Little Christmas

Peek through the window on a cold winter night
and you'll see a tree with thousands of lights.

Ornaments glisten in gold, green and red.
Around the tree a garland is thread.

Cookies and milk are left on a table
for Santa to eat as soon as he's able.

St. Nick leaves us presents then doesn't delay
to fly with his reindeer up high in his sleigh.

Stockings that hang near a cozy, warm fire
soon have been filled for each child's desire.

All fast alseep until Christmas morn,
everyone's merry when we wake up that dawn.

I Put Pen to Paper
James Boucher

When I put pen to paper
I feel a surge of energy flow within me
and down to the paper
forming into words.

Emotions and thoughts flood my mind,
spinning, rolling like a tornado,
spreading its wrath across the face of the page.
When I put pen to paper

I take a deep, slow breath,
relaxing my arm, hand and mind.
I let go of the sounds around me,
focusing only on myself.

When I put pen to paper
I feel that nothing in the world can break
me away from all my thoughts, feelings
and the words that make all these poems flow.

When I put pen to paper I'm free.

Melissa is a naturally quiet person. She has been writing poetry as a way to open up her heart to others so they might understand how much she cares about people. She is working on a book of her own poems. You can learn more about Melissa on page 52.

Light
Melissa Angilly

The light is me
Light comes in the window
I care like the light

Each year in April on **"Poem in Your Pocket Day,"** *the American Academy of Poets encourages people around the country to select a poem, carry it with them, and share it.*

You can find the Poem-in-Your-Pocket date for this year, and also download a poem to carry at: www.poets.org/national-poetry-month/poem-your-pocket-day

We enjoy the yearly celebration and hope you'll join us. Last year, one of our own collaborators celebrated her inner bard by writing this poem on the facing page.

After you've read Diane's poem, turn the page to find our favorite poems for your pocket from the Academy of American Poets. And read more about Diane on page 72.

A Poem for a Pocket
Diane S.

Beatnik beetles listen
to poems.
Read aloud from antique
tomes.
Frogs and crickets enjoy
the rhyme
Creaking and cheeping along
in time.
Woodland creatures love
poetry class
While jazz is played on
gleaming brass
Saxophone sizzles along
with words
Melodies rise from singing
birds.
Bumblebee drinks from
a margarita glass.
Ladybug sips tea
with dainty class.
All feel sad when
the poetry ends.
Poems are best when
shared with friends.

Stopping by Woods on a Snowy Evening
Robert Frost

Whose woods these are I think I know.
His house is in the village though;
He will not see me stopping here
To watch his woods fill up with snow.

My little horse must think it queer
To stop without a farmhouse near
Between the woods and frozen lake
The darkest evening of the year.

He gives his harness bells a shake
To ask if there is some mistake.
The only other sound's the sweep
Of easy wind and downy flake.

The woods are lovely, dark and deep.
But I have promises to keep,
And miles to go before I sleep,
And miles to go before I sleep.

This poem is in the public domain.

Untitled
Rudyard Kipling

You mustn't swim till you're six weeks old,
Or your head will be sunk by your heels;
And summer gales and Killer Whales
   Are bad for baby seals.
Are bad for baby seals, dear rat,
   As bad as bad can be.
But splash and grow strong,
And you can't be wrong,
Child of the Open Sea!

This poem is in the public domain.

Clouds
Christina Rossetti

White sheep, white sheep,
On a blue hill,
When the wind stops,
You all stand still.
When the wind blows,
You walk away slow.
White sheep, white sheep,
Where do you go?

The Good Moolly Cow [excerpt]
Eliza Lee Follen

Come! supper is ready;
Come! boys and girls, now,
For here is fresh milk
From the good moolly cow.

Have done with your fife,
And your row de dow dow,
And taste this sweet milk
From the good moolly cow.

When children are hungry,
O, who can tell how
They love the fresh milk
From the good moolly cow!

So, when you meet moolly,
Just say, with a bow,
"Thank you for your milk,
Mrs. Good Moolly Cow."

The Lake Isle of Innisfree
W. B. Yeats

I will arise and go now, and go to Innisfree,
And a small cabin build there, of clay and wattles made:
Nine bean-rows will I have there, a hive for the honey-bee;
And live alone in the bee-loud glade.

And I shall have some peace there, for peace comes dropping slow,
Dropping from the veils of the morning to where the cricket sings;
There midnight's all a glimmer, and noon a purple glow,
And evening full of the linnet's wings.

I will arise and go now, for always night and day
I hear lake water lapping with low sounds by the shore;
While I stand on the roadway, or on the pavements grey,
I hear it in the deep heart's core.

Dear Friends
Edwin Arlington Robinson

Dear friends, reproach me not for what I do,
Nor counsel me, nor pity me; nor say
That I am wearing half my life away
For bubble-work that only fools pursue.
And if my bubbles be too small for you,
Blow bigger then your own: the games we play
To fill the frittered minutes of a day,
Good glasses are to read the spirit through.

And whoso reads may get him some shrewd skill;
And some unprofitable scorn resign,
To praise the very thing that he deplores;
So, friends (dear friends), remember, if you will,
The shame I win for singing is all mine,
The gold I miss for dreaming is all yours.

Photography

Photos on pages 30, 32, 34-36, 50, 52-56, 58, 59, 61, 62, 64-69, 71 and 73 by **Rachel McKenna**.

page 51 photo properrty of Carol Anderheggen
pages 57, 70 photos: via Visualhunt.com
page 60 photo property of Helen D'Ordine
page 63, eccentricvirgo via Visualhunt.com
page 72 photo: catlovers via Visualhunt.com

Thursdays at 2
Poets

Fred A

Fred has worked at Walmart for 17 years as a greeter. He also helps deliver flowers for West Bay. He is a big TV fan, especially enjoys watching vintage game shows like "Let's Make A Deal" and the shows on TVLand. He loves meatballs and his favorite color is blue. He has been dating his girlfriend Carol for 7 years and loves going out with her. The poetry group on Thursdays has encouraged him to speak up and offer suggestions. He has learned to appreciate the process of creating a poem.

Carol Anderheggen

Carol is a member of Ocean State Poets, a non-profit organization dedicated to the promotion and sharing of poetry. Their mission is "To bring the transformative nature of poetry to Rhode Islanders by encouraging reading, writing and sharing poetry and to create opportunities for others to find their own voices." Her poems have appeared in *The Great Swamp Gazette*, *The 2010 Rhode Island Writer's Circle Anthology*, *URI Women*, *Anemone*, *Northeast Journal* and many other regional journals. She has self-published two chapbooks – *Are You a Born Child?* and *The Breast Cycle, a Journey of Dreams and Nightmares*. Carol facilitated the Cycle of Life Haiku on page 31.

Melissa Angilly

Melissa is very interested in healthy eating, and enjoys sharing her knowledge with others. She cares deeply about everyone's health and happiness, enjoys hanging out with her boyfriend Tim, and loves to make other people feel good. She expresses her caring through writing and art. She has written a book in which she lists the positive qualities of many of the people who have come into her life. One of her poems is featured on page 39.

Mark has provided data entry assistance for several projects at West Bay including tracking supply orders (for the homes). Personally he has sold collectibles on E-bay. In his free time, Mark likes to browse the Internet, shop at the Warwick Mall and enjoys eating at Chinese and Italian restaurants. He enjoys all types of movies and spending time with his sisters during holidays. Mark's favorite thing to do is to spend time on his computer, especially playing games. He finds this relaxing and a bit of an escape. Prior to the Thursdays at Two group, Mark had not read poetry and says he did not realize how much he would enjoy writing poetry. He says, "I hadn't realized how imaginative it could be."

Rachel loves to go to movies and hang out with her friends and her boyfriend. She's a huge Dunkin Donuts fan, and enjoys trying out new flavors of coffee.

Gloria volunteers delivering Meals on Wheels. Her dream job would be to work at a school. She enjoys people and loves children! She also likes music and going out for coffee, tea or lunch/dinner with friends. She especially enjoys the company of her dog Sammy.

James Boucher

James was a past member of the West Bay Residential Services Board of Directors, and holds a job as an administrative assistant, collating day activities packets for all of the group homes supported by West Bay. He is currently writing his memoir, to be published by Rose Hall Media Company in October of 2016. James is also the man who came up with the idea of making collaborative poetry at West Bay. In 1996 he was awarded the Ginsberg Prize for his poem, *I Put Pen to Paper* (page 38). His memoir will be published by Rose Hall Media Company in October, 2016.

Laura has been part of the West Bay team for five years. In her free time she likes to exercise, watch anything on Bravo! and hold her baby girl.

Corinne Charlette

Before Corinne retired, she was employed in a workshop. Now she likes to watch movies, especially romance and comedy, and she loves to spend time with her friends. Being a nice person is important to her, and everyone who knows her agrees that she is!

Katie is a fan of Disney movies, singing and dancing. She loves fashion and glamour--the more bling, the better. One of her favorite things is to have weekend visits with her dad.

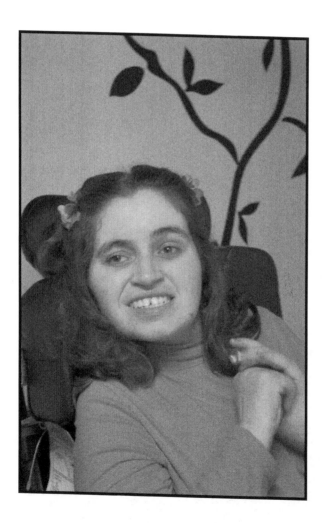

Helen D'Ordine.

Not many people know that Helen wrote a clue card for the board game, CLEVER ENDEAVOR. She is a retired teacher and former adjunct professor at Rhode Island College, a former member of The Writers' Circle, and a Rhode Island Writing Project Fellow. Helen is currently an Ocean State Poet, an Origami Poet, and has attended the Block Island Poetry Project for ten years. Her chapbook, CONCLUSIVE ILLUSIONS was published in 2011. She's had poems published in Mobius, RI Writers' Circle Anthology, The Providence Journal:Poetry Corner, sheShines, Medicine & Health/ RI, the Block Island Poetry Project's 10 year Anniversary Anthology, and twice at the Poetry and Art Exhibit of the Wickford Art Association. Helen facilitated the poem on page 12.

Jodie enjoys delivering flowers to one of our local radio stations. She has also assisted with a coffee delivery service. She likes relaxing and watching a good movie. Some of her favorite things are having her fingernails painted, shopping, and people watching. Jodie likes any sweet food, especially pancakes and cantaloupe, but she likes carrots too. Red is her favorite color. Jodie's friend Kathy says that Jodie's participation in the poetry group "makes me stop and appreciate beauty, like flowers and rain on a steamy, hot day".

Debbie Jette

Debbie is employed with the Books Are Fun program and delivers bread to the East Greenwich Community Center, as well as helps with the recycling program at West Bay. In her free time she likes to go out for coffee, play board games and UNO, and hang out with her boyfriend Dave.

Tracy is a writer, editor and creative arts educator. She began writing poetry when she was twelve, and holds an English Literature/Creative Writing degree from the University of Minnesota.

She blogs about artistic/creative expression, wellness, and tips for caregivers at

TracyLeeKarner.com

Cathy Keithan (cover artist)

Cathy works at Yard Works nursery and does landscaping around the West Bay office. In her free time, she loves computer games, gardening, Pinterest and keeping up with friends on Facebook. She also loves staying at friend's homes, going to the annual Flower Show in Providence, and attending the Rubber Stamp Show in Springfield, Massachusetts. She likes going to Paint and Vino classes. She could eat mac and cheese every day. If she had a favorite color it might be sky blue with clouds, or medium lavender. About her artwork, Cathy says, "Making art is relaxing and fun. I like drawing flowers and trying different techniques."

Hope enjoys getting her nails and her hair done, and loves coffee with cream and sugar. Her favorite color is purple.

Bruce Montgomery

Bruce volunteers for St. Luke's food pantry. He likes rock-and-roll music, going out with his family, and loves dancing to Billy Ray Cyrus' Achy-Breaky Heart. His favorite color is blue.

Rick has assisted with filling supply orders at the West Bay office for almost three years. He likes placing items in boxes, and enjoys listening to other workers around him. Some of his favorite things to do include puzzles, having a drink at Dunkin Donuts, and listening to classic rock music. He loves Italian food and his favorite color is blue. Rick enjoys gathering with others for Thursdays at 2. He is always very attentive during the poetry group session and likes the sharing of ideas.

Yvette Peck

Yvette has worked at West Bay for 21 years. She loves to read and exercise, and often leads the poetry-making session on Thursdays at 2.

John's favorite part of making poems together is what he learns—about people in the group, and about the world around us. When you find a cat or kitten in one of our poems, you can safely bet it showed up there because of John's input. In his free time, he likes to spend time with his parents and his girlfriend Rachael, play Gin Rummy and Uno, play Wii—especially Mario and Wheel of Fortune—do word puzzles, and watch movies from his DVD collection.

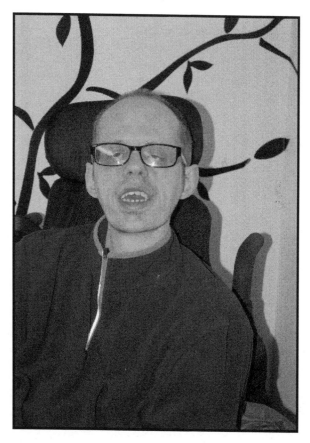

RaeAnn R

RaeAnn has been part of the West Bay team for three years. In her free time she enjoys listening to music and hanging out with her five-year-old daughter.

Susan is the Employment & Inclusion Specialist at West Bay. She was awarded "Direct Support Professional of the Year" in 2014 and the "Excellence in Service" award in 2016. She has been a member of the West Bay team for 22 years and likes to joke that she began working when she was only five. Relationships are extremely important to her. In her free time she likes to get together with a handful of friends. She believes in having fun and staying active, and enjoys exercising, cooking, and healthy eating.

Diane has worked at West Bay for over 25 years. In her free time, she likes to read and do artwork. She began to enjoy poetry as a young student in school, but did not write poems until Thursdays at 2 at West Bay sparked her interest. She has recently begun leading a poetry class at a local nursing home, where the residents love painting with words and sharing their creative ideas.

Arthur works in housekeeping. In his free time he likes to shop, play video games, go out to eat (his favorite food is Chinese), and go to the library to check out books and movies. Although he is proud of being smart, he tries to show friendliness and helpfulness to everyone he meets, because these qualities are very important to him.

How to use this book
to write collaborative poetry
with your group

1. Begin by understanding your goal. You are trying to bring your group's unique, individual talents together in collaboration to make poems. Poetry can help us appreciate the wonder, joy and love wrapped up in our daily experiences. It can open our eyes to the important, mysterious truth that although there are superficial differences in our appearances, abilities, thoughts and opinions, in our essential humanity all of us are very much the same.

2. All you need to know is that poetry uses ordinary words, but strings them together in surprising ways, with images and metaphors. Images are words that cause our imaginations to see, hear, taste, smell and feel. Metaphors are words that connect an ordinary thing to an image. For example "hugs that taste like butterscotch and raindrops."

3. Choose a poem from this book and read it to your group.

4. Use the description on the page facing the poem to inspire a question you can ask the group. Your job is to ask interesting questions, then write down your group's responses on a white board or large presentation tablet of paper.

5. Ask questions that end with the word *like*. For example: *what does that look like? smell like? sound like? taste*

like? feel like? Or, if your group has trouble with abstract concepts (people who have cognitive processing disabilities), ask them *what's your favorite sweet (sour, salty) food? favorite color? name something soft (slippery, cold)? what smells make you happy? what else in the world is blue (green, purple...)?*

6. Perhaps pick a key word someone has said, and ask for rhyming words. On a separate sheet of paper, or on another section of the board, write those words. Now go back to your topic/the poem you're working on, and ask the group for sentences or phrases that use those words. (Rhymes don't have to come at the end of a line; they can be anywhere in the poem).

7. Perhaps make a list of words that describe the color, texture, smell, taste, and sound of an object or place. Plug the best of those into your poem.

8. Appreciate each contribution! Say "good one!" "thank you!" "that's so interesting!" "I never would have thought of that!" "yes!" "beautiful!" If you sincerely value and give reverent attention to every participant, your group will learn to see and listen to one another more carefully. This will build deeper, more respectful relationships.

9. Most importantly, just laugh and have fun!

to enjoy more poetry
visit these websites:

poets.org

poems.com

Made in the USA
Middletown, DE
31 August 2016